Joshua's Egg

A Play for Children

Jacqui Shapiro

A SAMUEL FRENCH ACTING EDITION

SAMUEL FRENCH

FOUNDED 1830

SAMUELFRENCH-LONDON.CO.UK
SAMUELFRENCH.COM

ISBN 978-0-573-05119-7

www.samuelfrench-london.co.uk

www.samuelfrench.com

JOSHUA'S EGG

The play was commissioned by Theatre Centre. The first performance was at the Mercury Theatre, Colchester on 2nd May 1997 with the following cast:

Joshua	Arnie Hewitt
Helen/Lucy	Flo Wilson
Martin/Uncle Ronnie	Jon Samuel
Auntie Peggy/Mama Maiasaura	Amanda Lawrence

Directed by Peter Rumney
Designed by Lou Gray

CHARACTERS

Joshua, six years old
Helen, his mother
Martin, his father
Lucy, five years old
Auntie Peggy, Joshua's friend, a weaver of magic
Uncle Ronnie, Joshua's uncle and Martin's brother, a
    "businessman"
Mama Maiasaura, a mother dinosaur

Doubling (if necessary)

Helen/Lucy
Martin/Uncle Ronnie
Auntie Peggy/Mama Maiasaura

AUTHOR'S NOTE

Joshua's Egg was conceived as a play for four adult actors (with some doubling), a minimal, touring set and no lighting. It played in schools and small theatre venues, and although it was aimed at audiences aged between five and seven, it was also successful with older audiences, up to the age of about ten or eleven.

Joshua's Egg is a story about a child coming to terms with his world through play and through the use of his imagination. Therefore we don't need to see "real"dinosaurs or a concrete, realistic time machine, but dinosaurs and time travel seen through the eyes of a six-year-old. The play and indeed Joshua, the central character, both walk a thin line between reality and fantasy and Theatre Centre's production reflected this.

We discovered early on in the rehearsal process that the most effective dinosaur was one created by an actor "becoming" one using movement, without recourse to elaborate costumes or props. A choreographer worked extensively with the actors to create convincing dinosaurs in the scene set in prehistory. In fact the start of the scene became a kind of set piece, in which all the actors played dinosaurs. Similarly, the time travel sequence was devised using acrobatic movement, and, very importantly, recorded sound.

Sound played a crucial role in the Theatre Centre production, with over fifty sound cues (some literal, some representational) creating atmosphere and a sense of time and place. The location of each section is almost immediately apparent through the dialogue, so there is no need for elaborate scenery.

Changes of location and jumps in time were signalled through the use of sound. (You could use lighting if you have some.) To signal the end of a section, the actors would freeze briefly before making necessary changes of props or scenery as part of the action, so the play flowed smoothly from one part to the next.

The production capitalized on the medium of theatre, encouraging its audience to use their imaginations to do what children do so expertly — to bridge the gap between representation and reality.

Jacqui Shapiro

MUSIC

The music for the four songs in this play can be found at the back of this book, pp. 35-44.

Copies of the music in A4 format are available on free loan from Samuel French Ltd.

A CD of backing tracks and vocal guides for the songs is available on hire from Samuel French Ltd.

Please contact our Librarian.

For Jacob

With many thanks to Rosamunde Hutt and all the staff at Theatre Centre; Peter Rumney; and my patient and inspiring family.

JOSHUA'S EGG

Joshua's bedroom

Joshua's bed is a large beanbag; all the other furniture is imaginary. The room has been turned into a prehistoric forest, with lots of model dinosaurs. Books about dinosaurs, model paints and brushes and various toys — a hoop, a skateboard, a bendy plastic pipe and a toy spade — are close at hand (perhaps in a box tucked away unobtrusively)

Joshua, age six, and his mother Helen, who is heavily pregnant, are playing a game about dinosaurs

Joshua Imagine there's a huge, scary dinosaur, a tyrannosaurus rex, sniffing around for food. (*He pretends to be the tyrannosaurus and roars off into the distance*)

Helen And imagine there's a mother dinosaur, a maiasaura, hiding from it in the jungle ——

Joshua And pretend that luckily the tyrannosaurus rex sees a whole herd of plant-eating dinosaurs in the distance and runs after them, roaring ——

Helen And pretend that the mother maiasaura comes out of the jungle, goes over to her nest, and begins to cover her egg with leaves ——

Joshua And pretend that a hungry oviraptor is watching the mother from behind a giant palm tree and he knows where the egg is and he wants to eat it — and pretend that when the maiasaura goes away to get a drink of water from the swamp ... Go on, Mum ...

Helen heaves herself to her feet and goes towards the window

No, Mum! The swamp's on the bed, Mum, on the bed ——

Helen pretends to drink from the pretend swamp

— and pretend that while the mother is away, the oviraptor scampers over to the nest and picks up the egg in its mouth ... (*He runs to the nest, picks up the pretend egg in his mouth and runs away*)

Martin, Joshua's father, comes in and watches Helen and Joshua

Helen And pretend that when the mother came back and found her egg was gone, she went like this … (*She lets rip with a blood-curdling roar*)

Joshua looks on admiringly

Joshua Good roar, Mum …
Martin Hey, Josh, your mum's looking tired. Why not give her a little break?
Joshua She doesn't need a break, do you, Mum?
Helen Come to think of it, I'm starving. What's for tea?
Martin Dino-burgers, prehistoric potato parcels and fried ferns.
Joshua But what about the maiasaura's egg? We have to finish the game …
Helen Tomorrow.
Joshua Promise?
Helen Promise.
Martin Pretend I was a great big cuddleosaurus and I gave you a great big cuddle …
Joshua No. Pretend we were a family of hungry maiasauras preparing for tea … (*He stomps around, making dinosaur noises*)

His parents look at each other and sigh

Come on …

Helen and Martin look at each other again, shrug and stomp around roaring behind Joshua

Night comes

   Martin and Helen exit

Joshua goes to bed and falls asleep

   Helen comes in

Helen Joshua … Joshua … Can you hear me?

Joshua sleepily nods his assent

   Listen, the doctor says I have to go into hospital for a few days …
Joshua (*sitting up*) Hospital? Are you going to have an operation?
Helen No. She says I just need bed rest.
Joshua But you promised we'd finish the game.
Helen And we will. When I come home.
Joshua But you said we'd finish it tomorrow. You've broken a promise.

There is the sound of a car hooter

Helen That's your dad.
Joshua Dad? Then who's going to look after me?

Uncle Ronnie comes in

Uncle Ronnie Hi, Josh. It's me. Uncle Ronnie.
Joshua Uncle Ronnie?
Ronnie Your dad asked me to keep an eye on you while your mum's away.
Joshua Are you sure?
Ronnie We've always been good mates, haven't we? We're going to have a smashing time together, you and I.
Joshua Can't Dad look after me?
Helen He'll take some holiday after the baby's born.

The hooter sounds again

Ronnie leaves

Give us a great big sloppy kiss.

Joshua turns away

You can visit me in hospital.

Joshua doesn't respond. Helen kisses him

Helen exits

Joshua Why's she having a stupid baby anyway? (*He goes back to sleep*)

Morning comes

Joshua is reading a book about dinosaurs

Lucy comes in and examines Joshua's dinosaur collection

Joshua is engrossed in his reading and doesn't see her immediately

Joshua Who are you?
Lucy My room's much bigger than this and I've got a bunk bed. I can play the guitar and the drums and the piano. What can you play?
Joshua Dad! Dad!

Lucy (*looking at the dinosaurs*) Wow. Look at all these. (*She picks up a dinosaur and looks at it admiringly*) This is really cool.

Joshua (*jumping to his feet*) Get off. That's my baryonyx walkeri. It's a limited edition.

Lucy Baryonyx whateri?

Joshua Walkeri. Mum gave it to me for my birthday. Please replace it where you found it.

Lucy Why should I?

Joshua It's mine! Give it to me!

Lucy Try and get it then!

Joshua tries to grab the dinosaur from Lucy. Lucy holds it high above her head where Joshua can't reach it. He tackles her and the dinosaur breaks

Joshua Dad!

Ronnie comes in and takes in the scene

Uncle Ronnie, where's Dad?

Ronnie Oh dear, oh dear, oh dear, oh dear, oh dear.

Lucy We can glue it.

Joshua Shut up!

Ronnie Oh dear, oh dear, oh dear, oh dear.

There is a pause. Joshua looks at his broken dinosaur

Lucy (*to Joshua*) I'm really sorry.

Joshua Do your parents know you're here?

Ronnie They're away, aren't they Lucy? She's staying next door with my friend Sandra.

Lucy My Auntie Sandra.

Ronnie Sandra asked me to look after her. I'm great with kids. Lucy's a bit down in the dumps with her parents gone, so ——

Lucy No I'm not. My mum and dad are in a rock band. They're very famous. Are your parents famous?

Joshua No. But my mum plays the best games in the world and my dad can fix anything. Dad! Dad!

Ronnie He had to go to work early.

Joshua Good. Good. I'm really glad.

Lucy You don't look glad.

Joshua Look, I didn't invite you, did I?

Ronnie Come on, Lucy. Come downstairs and have a chocolate biscuit.

Lucy Yeah. Cool. (*To Joshua*) It could be worser. Your dad's only at work.
Mine's in Australia.

Ronnie and Lucy head for the exit

(*To Ronnie*) You know what? The postman might bring a letter from my
mum today.

They exit

*Joshua is left holding his broken dinosaur. He carefully puts it down. Then
he climbs on to the bed, strikes the pose of a tyrannosaurus rex*

Joshua (*roaring loudly*) I'm a tyrannosaurus rex and I'm very, very angry!
(*He prowls around until he finds a toy maiasaura and pretends to devour
it in the most disgusting way possible*)

Some time passes

*Joshua takes out paints, a brush and a model dinosaur; he begins to paint the
dinosaur*

  Lucy enters carrying a small electric piano

Song: I Don't Need A Friend

Lucy (*playing the piano and singing*)
> I'll sing you a song of my mother
> And the millions of letters she sends
> She writes to me twice
> Ev'ry day, which is nice
> In all of the world
> I'm her specialest girl
> So I certainly don't need
> I def'nitely don't need
> I certainly don't — don't need a friend.
>
> I'll sing you a song of my father
> Of the magical hours we spend
> Singing songs, playing games
> Thinking up silly names
> Eating hot buttered toast
> 'Cos he loves me the most
> So I certainly don't need

I def'nitely don't need
I certainly don't — don't need a friend.

I'll sing you a song about Lucy
A girl who knows how to pretend
But I'm missing my mum
And the post doesn't come
When it does it's not there
No, the letter's … not there
But I certainly don't need
I def'nitely don't need
I certainly don't — don't need a friend.

I'll sing you a song of my mother ——

Joshua Lucy, stop making that infernal racket! I'm trying to concentrate!

Lucy This is not a infernal racket, this is a song about love!

Joshua Well, I don't like love and I don't like the song! It sounds like a herd of triceratops banging their horns together!

Lucy No, it doesn't! It sounds like a herd of pianosauruses having a party. You don't know anything about music!

Joshua And you don't know anything about dinosaurs! There's no such thing as a pianosaurus! And dinosaurs didn't have parties!

Lucy How do you know? You weren't even there!

Joshua Right, that's it. (*He heads out of the room*)

Lucy What are you doing? Where are you going?

Joshua Garden.

Lucy Can I come?

Joshua No.

Lucy What shall I do then?

Joshua Can't you go back to your auntie's?

Lucy She's having a nap.

Joshua Another one?

Lucy She wants me out of the house.

Joshua Look, I don't care what you do, but don't you dare touch my dinosaurs.

Lucy exits

Joshua goes out into the garden, which is covered in snow. He begins to dig in the snow

I wish there was a place where I could live by myself. On the moon. Or under the sea. Or … or millions of years back in time, before human beings even existed. Yes, I could go and live with the dinosaurs. Nobody would find me there. (*Suddenly he notices something in the place where he has been digging. He gets excited. He digs and digs until he exposes a very large, speckled egg*) No — it can't be. It can't be! It is! I've found a dinosaur egg! (*He carefully touches the egg. He leans down and puts his ear to it. He tries very hard to lift it but it is stuck fast in the ice*) Hey! Lucy! Uncle Ronnie! I've found a dinosaur egg! Uncle Ronnie! Lucy! I've found a — — (*He claps his hand to his mouth and shakes his head*)

Lucy laughs, off; we hear Ronnie chasing her

Joshua hastily covers the egg with snow

Lucy arrives brandishing Ronnie's mobile phone

Lucy You can't catch me!

Ronnie arrives, puffing and exhausted

Hey, d'you know the number for Australia?
Ronnie No! Now Lucy, for the last time, give that back!
Lucy Can I stay for tea?
Ronnie Yes, yes, anything — anything you say …

Lucy gives Ronnie the phone

Thank you. Thank you, Lucy.
Lucy What shall we do now?
Ronnie Tell you what, let's go down the market. Kids are meant to eat vegetables, aren't they?
Joshua Great. I can go and see Auntie Peggy. (*To Lucy*) She's got a stall with magic things. She's very old. Guess how old she is. Go on, guess.
Lucy Fourteen?
Joshua Don't be stupid. Fourteen isn't even grown up. She's so old, she used to look after Uncle Ronnie and Dad when they were children. Come on. I'll race you.

They exit

Joshua runs to the market

Lucy tries to keep up with Joshua, but she falls behind and exits

Auntie Peggy enters and meets Joshua

Peggy There's magic about you this morning, boy. I can smell it.

Joshua I was in the garden and I found this dinosaur egg and I've got to put it inside because it needs to get warm, so that the baby inside can grow and when it's grown it'll hatch and when it's hatched I'll have a prehistoric pet all of my very own.

Peggy Oh dear.

Joshua And I'll call it Joshuasaurus. Because I found it.

Peggy Dinosaurs can be very dangerous, you know.

Joshua Not baby ones.

Peggy Babies grow.

Joshua I thought you'd be pleased.

Peggy Has it occurred to you that the egg might have a mother?

Joshua Well, no, not exactly.

Peggy And have you any idea how angry a mother can get if someone tries to steal her young?

Joshua But the mother must have perished millions of years ago …

Peggy Have you ever heard of time travel?

Joshua Time travel?

Peggy If that mother really wants her baby, she may decide to come and get it.

Joshua You're bonkers.

Peggy Am I? Am I really? We'll see about that. (*She goes into a trance-like state*) Take me back, back, back through the mists of time to the age of the dinosaurs … Yes, yes … I see it now, the brown earth, the giant palms, the blue sky — I've never seen a sky so blue — and in the distance a vast swamp — and beneath the trees a fully grown female lies next to an empty nest …

Joshua Where? Where? I can't see anything …

Peggy Oh, no. There's something wrong. Can you hear? She's howling for her baby… what a terrible sound! … Oh! Oh! (*She draws back suddenly, in horror*)

Joshua What's the matter?

Peggy She looked at me! And then she looked at you. It's never happened before …

Joshua Please don't. It's not funny.

Peggy Indeed it is not. Now she knows where you are.

Joshua So what if she does?

Peggy If I were you I'd leave that egg alone …

Joshua and Auntie Peggy part

Auntie Peggy exits

Night comes

Joshua goes out to the garden with his toy spade and begins to dig

Lucy appears at her window next door, clutching her hot water bottle and watching Joshua

Joshua doesn't see Lucy. He tries to hack at the ice around the egg

Lucy Hiya! I couldn't sleep. I keep thinking about the letter from Mum. Auntie Sandra says it could have got displayed in the post.
Joshua You mean delayed, Lucy, delayed.
Lucy What are you doing?
Joshua Sshh! Keep your voice down! I'm just digging.
Lucy What for?
Joshua Nothing. Nothing.
Lucy Wait there. I'm coming out. (*She emerges from her house and scampers through the hedge, still clutching her hot water bottle. She sees the egg*) Wow.
Joshua Yeah?
Lucy That's an egg.
Joshua Possibly.
Lucy And I bet I know what's going to pop out of that egg. I bet I do. A dinosaurus. That's what. A baby dinosaurus.
Joshua Dinosaur. Not dinosaurus.

Lucy approaches the egg

Don't touch it. It's mine.
Lucy It's stuck in the ice, isn't it? You can't get it out, can you? Well if you promise to share it with me, I'll tell you how to unstick it.
Joshua You? Don't be ridiculous.

Song: Adventures With Lucy

Lucy (*singing*)   I'm only five and a quarter
                         My name is Lucy Snow
                         You think I'm just a baby
                         But you should know all the things I know-ow
Joshua (*speaking*) Sshhh! You'll wake the grown-ups!
Lucy (*singing*)   You can own a skateboard
                         Or any toy you like
                         But adventures aren't for owning
                         Like your Lego set or three-speed bike
                         You've got to take somebody with you
                         Now who could that somebody be?

Joshua (*speaking*) No idea.
Lucy (*singing*)   Adventures are better
                         With Lucy
                         You've met her
                         She's me!

                         Batman — he's got Robin
                         Or he wouldn't be brave and bold
                         Even Supergirl gets nervous
                         Without a friendly hand to ho-old

                         Certain to get lonely
                         Or frightened in the end
                         But if you share your adventure I promise
                         I'll be your bestest friend

                         You've got to take somebody with you
                         Now who could that somebody be?
                         Adventures are better
                         With Lucy
                         You've met her
                         She's me!

Joshua ⎫   You've got to take somebody with you
Lucy   ⎭   And something is telling me who
                       Adventures are better
                       With Lucy
Joshua   I've met her
                       She's you!

Lucy Watch this. (*She lays her hot water bottle down in the snow next to the egg*)

Joshua That's quite clever actually. The ice is beginning to melt. We'll have the egg out in no time. (*He starts digging around the egg*)

Lucy Where shall we keep it?

Joshua It has to be somewhere warm so it can thaw. Strictly speaking, someone should sit on it till it hatches.

Lucy Well I'm not going to.

Joshua I didn't ask you. We'll secrete it inside my wardrobe. I'll cover it with sweaters and things.

The egg is freed from the ice. Joshua picks it up

Lucy It doesn't sound very safe to me. Anyone could find it.

Joshua You think you know everything, don't you? My wardrobe is the safest place in the whole universe for this egg.

Lucy exits

Joshua goes inside the house and carefully puts the egg in his (imaginary) wardrobe, covering it with some (real) clothes

Day comes

Uncle Ronnie enters with a pile of neatly-folded washing

Uncle Ronnie Laundry service.
Joshua No! I mean I'll do it.
Uncle Ronnie I folded this myself. You'll just chuck it in any old how.
Joshua I won't! I'll be extra careful.
Uncle Ronnie (*opening the wardrobe*) Look, I was a boy once and I know exactly what ——

Uncle Ronnie's mobile phone suddenly rings a very loud, piercing ring

(*Answering the phone*) Hi. Yes, Ted. ... Yes. ... Yes. ... I sold him what? ... Oh, yes, I remember. ... What? He called me a what? ... A thief? Look, you tell him from me they don't call me Honest Ron for (*he notices the egg*) — nothing. Sorry Ted, got to go — got to go ... (*He switches off the phone and lifts up the egg*)
Joshua My football?
Ronnie Funny shape for a football.
Joshua It's gone a bit flat.
Ronnie (*weighing the egg in his hand*) A bit heavy for a football, too.
Joshua That's because it's — it's an underwater football.
Ronnie An underwater football, eh? (*He gets ready to kick the egg*) Fancy a game?
Joshua No!
Ronnie I thought not. Sit down, sonny. Now listen. Your Uncle Ronnie wasn't born yesterday. I know an egg when I see one.
Joshua You do?
Ronnie When I was a boy, I was an expert on dinosaurs. I knew the difference between a diplodocus and a gallimimus, I could tell you the dimensions of a stegosaurus and I knew my Jurassic from my Cretaceous. Now, I'm a bit rusty, but if I'm not mistaken, this is a dinosaur egg and do you know what's going to hatch from this dinosaur egg?
Joshua A baby dinosaur.

Ronnie Exactly. Now. Have you ever wanted to be rich beyond your wildest dreams?

Joshua Be careful ——

Ronnie Because this little beauty could make us a lot of money.

Joshua But it's a secret ...

Ronnie Picture the scene ... Crowds of people flock to see the spectacle of the century. A genuine, living, breathing huge, gigantic, enormous — Ronnieasaurus in the world's first dinosaur circus!

Joshua Shouldn't it be Joshuasaurus?

Ronnie And think of the merchandizing potential. Ronnieasaurus T-shirts, Ronnieasaurus biscuits, remote-controlled Ronnieasaurus ...

Joshua No. Sorry, Uncle Ronnie, but no. I think the Joshuasaurus would be much happier staying at home with me ...

Ronnie Oh, there won't be room for a dinosaur in the house. Not with a new baby. They won't want any noisy dinosaurs around... or noisy little boys for that matter.

Joshua Oh, yes. Mum'll have her baby. I didn't consider that.

Ronnie Now if you promise to let me manage little Ronnieasaurus here, I promise to take you away from all this. What do you say? (*He holds out his hand*)

Joshua I can escape.

Joshua shakes Ronnie's hand

Ronnie Couldn't have put it better myself.

Ronnie puts Joshua to bed

Night-night. Sleep tight. Don't let the bed bugs bite.

Joshua goes to sleep

Suddenly a Maiasaura appears in the room with him

Maiasaura (*a low growl*) Grrr!

Joshua wakes slowly. He sits up, sees the Maiasaura and rubs his eyes

Up waking!

Joshua I don't want to. I'm having this great dream that there's a maiasaura in my bedroom.

Maiasaura Yes. Me. Maiasaura. Here. Bedroom.

Joshua Wow!

The Maiasaura howls longingly

Joshua What's the matter?
Maiasaura Egg-baby. (*She howls*)
Joshua What?
Maiasaura Egg-baby mine. I Mama.
Joshua So?
Maiasaura I losing. Joshua finding. Give to Mama.
Joshua If you loved it so much you shouldn't have left it.
Maiasaura You wrong. I good Mama. I covering egg with leaves. I going to swamp drinking water. I coming back, oviraptor stealing egg-baby. I chasing, but not enough fast. Oviraptor dropping egg-baby. I spending days and days looking for egg-baby in swamp, but egg-baby gone. Egg-baby gone!
Joshua Well hard luck. Egg-baby mine now.
Maiasaura Joshua!
Joshua Hey, you can't scare me.
Maiasaura (*receding into the background*) Joshua...
Joshua (*yawning*) Don't worry. Mama laying another egg-baby soon, and then you won't care about the first one any more — that's what always happens ... (*He turns over and goes to sleep*)

The Maiasaura exits

Day comes

Joshua gets up

   Martin enters with a bunch of flowers

Martin hands Joshua the flowers and they get into the lift in the hospital

Martin Floor four — floor five — floor six ... Here we are. Your mum's in there. She can't wait to see you. Here. Make yourself tidy. Now in you go.

The hospital room

   Helen enters and lies down on the beanbag under a sheet

Joshua pushes the door open, angrily

   Don't forget the flowers!

Joshua walks into the room and stands as far away from his mother as possible

Helen (*holding out her arms*) Josh!
Martin Go on, Joshua.
Joshua You broke a promise.
Helen Did I?
Joshua You promised to finish the game.
Helen Oh yes ... well, I will. I will. As soon as I get home.
Joshua You promised you'd finish the game the very next day.
Helen Look, love, sometimes people have to break promises. Now come and
   give me a hug.

Joshua doesn't move. Martin gives Joshua a little push

Martin Go on.
Joshua Uncle Ronnie wants to steal my egg.
Helen What egg?
Joshua And he keeps giving me Jaffa cakes.
Helen Oh, dear.
Joshua It's not funny.
Helen No, love.
Joshua And Lucy. That's another thing. She's always interfering. And when
   she's not interfering, she's singing.
Martin Mum'll be coming home soon.
Joshua Who says I want her to?
Helen What lovely flowers. Are they for me?
Joshua Dad's been working late every night.
Martin I tried to explain about that, Joshua. It's just ——
Joshua Just what? Just what? Why do grown-ups always do what they like
   and children always have to do what they're told? (*He flings the bunch of
   flowers on the floor*)
Martin Don't you talk to me like that!

Joshua walks away

  Helen exits

  The mother Maiasaura appears in front of Joshua

Maiasaura Is again me.
Joshua Go away!
Maiasaura You crying.

Joshua Joshua not crying.
Maiasaura You sad, me sad, egg-baby sad.
Joshua I don't care.
Maiasaura You wanting egg-baby die?
Joshua Die?
Maiasaura Egg-baby hatching soon. Egg go crack, crack. Baby crawling out looking Mama. No Mama. Baby crying, baby cold, baby hungry.
Joshua But Joshua making promise to Uncle Ronnie ——
Maiasaura Joshua only hatchling himself, too young looking after new-hatch baby. Joshua not enjoying to feeding baby, cleaning baby, licking baby …
Joshua Licking it? Yuck. I don't even like babies.
Maiasaura Please. I begging you. Only you having power to save Mama's egg-baby.
Joshua Look, I'll think about it, all right? I might let you take it. I might.
Maiasaura Mama no can take. Joshua bringing egg-baby to Mama.
Joshua What? How?
Maiasaura You building machine. Time machine. You taking egg-baby to Mama in time machine back, back, back, to time when Mama lay egg.
Joshua Me? I don't know how to build a time machine.
Maiasaura Maybe you needing some helpings.

Martin moves to Joshua

Joshua Helpings?
Martin I shouldn't have made you come. I'm sorry.
Maiasaura You not doing it alone. You asking friends for helpings. And fastly. Not much time left. (*She heads for the exit*)
Joshua Hey! Wait! How long have I got?
Martin Let's go home.
Maiasaura One moon-rise only. Many wishes of luck, hatchling.

The Maiasaura leaves

Joshua (*calling after the Maiasaura*) I'm not promising anything …
Martin (*feeling Joshua's forehead*) You feel a bit warm … Listen, there's good news. Mum's doing really well. She should be able to come back home tomorrow.
Joshua Tomorrow? Really?
Martin Yes.
Joshua Mum's coming home. That's brilliant, Dad. Mum's coming home! (*He hugs Martin*)
Martin Look, I'm sorry if I've been a bit tough on you, love.

Joshua Have you been missing Mum?
Martin You bet. Let's make her a welcome home cake, just you and me.
Joshua Actually Dad, I need to do some thinking. I've got a big decision to make.
Martin Yes?
Joshua Well, I found this dinosaur egg in the garden.
Martin Come on, let's go home.

Martin leads Joshua into the lift. Joshua stops

Joshua (*continuing his debate*) Uncle Ronnie wants to put the baby dinosaur in a circus, but I'd like to keep it as a pet. The only thing is, the mother, she's a maiasaura, she wants me to take it to her in a time machine. What do you think I should do, Dad?
Martin I think you should have an early night. I love you. Come on …
Joshua Perhaps I should ask Auntie Peggy …

Joshua goes back to his bedroom and picks up the egg

Martin exits

Auntie Peggy enters

Lucy enters, standing just outside the door, listening

Joshua All right, suppose I did decide to take the egg back. Suppose I did. I don't know how to build a time machine. Do you?
Peggy Well, I once wove a magic carpet, which is really the same sort of thing. You'll need help of course.
Joshua Oh no. Why?
Peggy You require concentrated magic for a mission of this magnitude, and a lot of it. And you'll need a companion for the journey.
Joshua You! You can come with me.
Peggy I wish I could. But my adventuring days are long gone. Oh, the things I did when I was a child — the places I went, the sights I witnessed on that magic carpet …
Joshua But who'll come with me then?

Lucy comes into the bedroom

Joshua (*giving the egg to Peggy*) Who let you in?
Lucy Back door was open.
Peggy Lucy. You're just in time.

Joshua How long have you been standing outside my room?

Lucy Oh, about twenty-ninety seconds.

Joshua Oh come off it, Lucy. There's no such number. Did you hear anything?

Lucy I put my fingers in my ears, like this. But I couldn't help it. I could give you some helpings like the mummysaura said.

Joshua Maiasaura, not mummysaura.

Lucy Anyway I didn't come to talk to you, I came to see our egg.

Joshua It's not our egg, it's *my* egg.

Lucy You know what, you're the meanest boy I've ever met!

Joshua And you're the — the interferingest girl!

Lucy No wonder you haven't got any friends.

Joshua No wonder your mum and dad went to Australia.

Lucy What do you mean?

Joshua They had to get away from you.

Pause

Lucy D'you want to know why your mum's having another baby? Because she doesn't love you any more!

The children are silent

Uncle Ronnie arrives

Ronnie So how's our little investment?

Peggy Not now, Ronald.

Ronnie Peggy, it's you.

Peggy Yes. Yes, it's me — and I don't need to tell you what I think about your plans, Ronald.

Ronnie What you think isn't what counts, though, is it, Peggy? It's what Joshua thinks that matters. And when he's seen my multi-media advertising campaign, he'll know I'm right.

Joshua What advertising campaign?

Ronnie Aha! (*He strikes a pose*)

Joshua Look, I'm not so sure any more.

Ronnie "Dino-baby! The show of the century! Marvel, as Dino-baby performs tap dancing routines, gasp as it flies through the air on its flying trapeze — and cease breathing altogether as Dino leaps through a hoop of real fire!"

Lucy You know what you are? You're a wicked, wicked man. Don't listen to him, Joshua.

Ronnie You! How did you get in here?

Lucy Don't you dare touch this egg!

Ronnie Now, now little girl ——

Lucy And I'm not a little girl! I'm five and a quarter. And my name is Lucy. And if this egg isn't taken back to its mother in a time machine, then the baby inside will die.

Ronnie (*to Joshua*) And what about your promise, eh?

Joshua Sometimes people have to break promises, don't they?

Ronnie Don't you want to be rich?

Joshua Rich?

Ronnie Look, lad. What you need is lots and lots of money because money makes the world go round ...

Joshua No, it doesn't. It's all to do with the movement of the planets.

Lucy But what about the time machine? What about the adventure? Going back to the voracious period? What about that?

Joshua Not voracious — Cretaceous!

Peggy gives Joshua the egg

Peggy Joshua, you have to make up your mind!

Lucy What about the adventure?

Ronnie And what about the money?

Joshua Oh, leave me alone, all of you!

Peggy, Ronnie and Lucy leave

Joshua (*to the egg*) Hi, egg-baby. This is Joshua speaking. You probably know my voice by now. Auntie Peggy says you can hear things through the shell. I bet you're really cute, aren't you? I've always wanted a pet. Your mum wants you back. But I want to keep you. I'm not your mum but I'll look after you very well. You won't even notice she isn't here. Mine's in hospital at the moment and I'm not missing her at all. I can look after myself. She's coming home today. I can't wait. We'll be able to ... we'll be able to ... Oh no, we won't. Mum's not the same as she used to be. We used to play together every day, me and my mum — I'm not crying, I've just got a bit of a cold ... and then Mum got pregnant and all of a sudden she was tired all the time and the other thing was, her lap disappeared. Her tummy got bigger and bigger and there wasn't any room on her lap for me; so you see mums aren't much use anyway ...

Martin comes in

Martin Look, Josh. I've only got a minute. Look. Look. Mum's doing really well, but she won't be home until after the baby's born. It's not the end of the world. It's due any day now.

Pause

Hey, don't cry.

Joshua I'm not crying. I've got something in my eye. Just because my mum's a liar, that doesn't mean I want to cry.

Martin tries to put his arms around Joshua. Joshua shrugs him off

She said she'd finish the game.

Martin I know. And she will.

Joshua But you said she was coming back today and I ——

Martin Look, I'm really sorry, Joshua. I have to ——

Joshua I know. Get back to work. You always have to get back to work but you never have to get back to me!

Martin Now you know that's not fair.

Joshua Well, don't bother to come back because I won't be here any more! I hate Jaffa cakes!

Martin leaves

I hate Uncle Ronnie! I hate Lucy! I hate Dad! I hate Mum! I hate dinosaurs! (*He lifts the egg high up above his head*) I hate babies!

Joshua brings the egg down, preparing to smash it on the floor

There is a sound of despair from the mother Maiasaura; then she appears once more in front of Joshua, protecting her egg

Maiasaura My egg-baby.

Joshua So?

Maiasaura So soft. You not hurting it. It can nothing do.

Joshua I hate babies.

Maiasaura You were baby once.

Joshua I can't remember that.

Maiasaura Everyone starting life as baby. Even Mama Maiasaura.

Joshua You?

Maiasaura And now I your friend. Egg-baby your friend. Please not hurting. Now hatchling. You putting egg down.

Joshua puts the egg down

Good hatchling. You having many workings to do. You starting building.

Joshua But how?

Maiasaura Using fine human brain.

Joshua But I'm only six.

Maiasaura Nothing largely difficult for you. I liking you. I liking you muchly.

Joshua Me?

Maiasaura Yes, you.

Joshua Look, it's your egg. Me wanting you have it. Me really do. But I don't know how to build a time machine ... Can't you help me? Please, don't go, don't go ...

The Maiasaura recedes

Lucy enters

Lucy Peggy says your mum's staying in hospital.

Pause

She made me and Ronnie a cup of tea. There's Jaffa cakes. I brought you one. (*She holds out a melted Jaffa cake in a chocolate covered hand*)

Joshua doesn't answer

D'you want to build a time machine?

Joshua doesn't answer

I'll help you if you like ...

Joshua Don't be stupid, Lucy. You're only five. You don't know anything about time machines...

Lucy Says who?

Song: Time Machine

(*Singing*)   I've been in a bus, flied on a plane
                     Been sick on a boat, thrown up on a train
                     I've even rided my bike in the rain
                     But there's something even better ——

Joshua (*speaking*) Yeah, what?

Lucy   Let me explain ...
                     You won't believe
                     The sights you'll see

In a time machine, time machine,
Time, time, time machine
You won't believe the sights you'll see
In a time machine
That goes whoosh, wham, whoosh, wham, wheeeeee!

If you want to see a real, live dinosaur
Use a time machine, 'cos that's what it's for
Press those buttons it'll go with a roar
Take you on a prehistoric tour ...

You won't believe
What you can do
In a time machine, time machine,
Time, time, time machine
You won't believe what you can do
In a time machine
That goes bim bam bim bam whoooo!

Sometimes I think sort of slow
'Cos I'm only five, but still I know
Some things you learn you've got to let go
Take egg to the Mama, let the baby grow ...

You won't believe
How far you flew
In a time machine, time machine,
Time, time, time machine
You won't believe how far you flew
In a time machine
That went bim bam bim bam whoooo!

Joshua }
Lucy }   You won't believe
How far you flew
In a time machine, time machine,
Time, time, time machine
You won't believe how far you flew
In a time machine
That went bim bam bim bam whoooo!

Joshua (*picking up the hoop and demonstrating*) Oh look, this hoop can be
  the rocket and it can go up and down like this ...
Lucy (*riding the skateboard*) And this can be the rocket launcher!

Joshua Sunglasses! Sunglasses, 'cos time travel is very bright. Lots of cosmic flashes.
Lucy And Jaffa cakes! 'Cos we can't eat giant palm trees like dinosaurs can …
Joshua (*getting the bendy plastic pipe*) And what's this for?
Lucy (*demonstrating*) Spacewalking!
Joshua Or it could be a seat belt! 'Cos the safety aspect is very important.

They continue to "build" their time machine and become very engrossed

Uncle Ronnie comes in. He picks up the egg and makes his way towards the door. Suddenly his mobile phone rings

Ronnie (*into the phone*) Not now, Ted!
Joshua Uncle Ronnie!
Ronnie Hi there, sonny. I was — er — I was just looking.
Lucy Stealing our egg, that's what you were doing. Stealing our egg.
Ronnie No, I wasn't. I was just keeping an eye on it.
Joshua Come on. Give it to me.
Ronnie Won't!

Suddenly there is the noise of an animal call, quite loud and distinct, but unfamiliar

Ronnie What was that?
Joshua I don't know.

The call comes again

Joshua It's coming from the egg. It's the baby dinosaur! That means it's going to hatch!
Ronnie Oh, I'm going to be rich! I'm going to be rich! At last!

Auntie Peggy arrives

The baby dinosaur calls again

Peggy Ronald, what are you doing?
Ronnie This is my dinosaur! It doesn't need its mother. It needs me.
Peggy Now you listen to me, young man. You may have forgotten, but I have not. You loved dinosaurs when you were a boy no older than Joshua himself. When you were ill as a child and you were sent to hospital, the only toy you took with you was your cuddly maiasaura. Bolly-Bom was his name.

Lucy Bolly-Bom?

Ronnie I don't know what you're talking about.

Peggy And the nurses said you used to lie in bed cuddling Bolly-Bom and
   crying for your mother as if your little heart would break …

Ronnie Yeah, well? So? That was a long time ago.

Lucy Uncle Ronnie …

Ronnie What?

Song: Think Back

Lucy (*singing*)   Think back to the time
                     When they sent you away
                     When you lay all alone
                     In a world, cold and grey
                     The pain in your heart
                     Was as big as the sky
                     You tried to be tough
                     But you wanted to cry

Lucy ⎫   Think back to the crying
Peggy ⎭   The time of stinging tears
                     And the child in the night
                     Who nobody hears
                     Remember the wanting,
                     The sobs and the sighs,
                     The echoing silence
                     That greeted his cries

Lucy ⎫   Think back to the boy
Peggy ⎬   And the man he became
Joshua ⎭   Who knows how to hear
                     A child who's in pain
                     The baby is calling
                     And here is the man
                     Who listens and waits
                     With its life in his hands

Lucy   Think back to the time ——
Ronnie   —— When they sent you away
Peggy   Think back to the time
Joshua   Think back to the time

Ronnie gives the egg to Joshua

Ronnie *Bon voyage*, sonnie.

Joshua Poor Uncle Ronnie…

Ronnie I'm not poor. You think I could afford to wear a suit like this if I was
poor?

The dinosaur calls again from inside the egg

Joshua It's shaking. It's shaking! I can feel the baby dinosaur moving inside.
We better hurry.

Joshua and Lucy climb into the time machine

Joshua Well, off we go then. Bye Auntie Peggy. Bye Uncle Ronnie.
Ronnie You know, Peggy, it's not very safe in prehistory.
Peggy No indeed, Ronald.
Ronnie I mean personally, I wouldn't go. There's all kinds of scary
things. With teeth. Big, scary things with teeth. I mean I don't want to
alarm you ——
Lucy You mean they might eat us?
Joshua I'm not scared.
Lucy Neither am I. Well, not really.
Ronnie (*climbing into the time machine*) You can't let kids wander around
all over prehistory without someone to keep an eye on them.
Joshua Bagsie me drive.
Lucy No way, José.
Joshua It's my egg!

Joshua pushes Lucy out of the way. She hits him

Ouch!

The dinosaur calls again

Lucy The magic demands co-operation or it simply won't work.
Joshua We'll both drive.
Lucy All right.

They both try to start the time machine. Nothing happens

Joshua Try again.

They try again. Again nothing happens

I knew we couldn't do it. We're only children. We were stupid to even think
it was going to work.

Ronnie Well, nobody can say we didn't try …

Ronnie, Joshua and Lucy climb out of the time machine. The dinosaur calls again

Lucy The baby's going to die without its mum and it'll be all our fault!
Peggy This is even harder than I thought. We're going to have to use the strongest magic I know. Now come along all of you and be quick about it.

Ronnie, Joshua and Lucy get back into the time machine and prepare for the journey through time

The baby will be born when the baby is ready. It isn't going to wait for anyone. You have to think of your imagination as the engine. And three engines are better than one. Now close your eyes. Cast your minds back, back through the mists of time, to the place where the mother is waiting for her egg. It's a swampy, marshy, damp, dangerous world where the sun shines dark and orange and the sky is blue as blue and the trees are the greenest green you can imagine …

They begin to move

Keep going! Don't stop imagining now!

They take off with a whoosh. They are whirled around and around until the time machine grinds to a halt in a prehistoric forest

A scene of live dinosaurs unfolds before them. Prehistoric creatures of all different types and sizes are all around them while, overhead, giant pterodactyls swoop and glide. They can hear many strange sounds

The egg cracks open and the baby dinosaur is born into Joshua's arms. Joshua, Lucy and Ronnie are amazed and delighted. The baby calls for its mother and we hear her answering cry

The mother Maiasaura enters through the giant trees and walks towards them. She takes her baby from Joshua, holding it with her mouth by the scruff of its neck

The mother Maiasaura leaves, and the baby dinosaur calls a last farewell to Joshua

No sooner have they gone, than a huge tyrannosaurus rex appears

Lucy Joshua…
Joshua Lucy…
Lucy Joshua, it's a… it's a tyrannosaurus rex!

*The tyrannosaurus opens and shuts its enormous jaws. Uncle Ronnie quickly
dials a number on his mobile phone. The tyrannosaurus comes closer*

Ronnie (*into the phone*) Hallo! Is that you, Peggy?… Yes, this is Ronald.
… Listen, can you please telephone me immediately on my mobile?…
Yes, now. It's a matter of life and death. (*He clicks the telephone shut*)

*The tyrannosaurus opens its enormous jaws. Lucy and Joshua turn and see
it. The telephone rings a loud, ear-splitting ring. The tyrannosaurus lets rip
with a bloodcurdling roar and runs away. Uncle Ronnie answers the phone*

(*Into the phone*) Thanks Auntie Peggy. We were nearly Monster Munch.
(*He clicks the phone shut and looks at the children*)

All is strangely quiet. Joshua and Lucy run into Ronnie's arms

Ronnie What's all this for then?
Joshua It's a hug.
Ronnie A hug?
Joshua Yes. Haven't you ever had one before?
Ronnie Not since I was a kid. My mum used to … You know, she used to
… Well, time to go home, I think. Who knows when that nasty tyranno-
saurus might come back.

Joshua looks around him, preoccupied

Lucy Joshua …
Joshua Hey, isn't it lovely?
Ronnie It's a bit hot and sticky.
Joshua If I explored a bit more, who knows what I might find …
Lucy But there aren't any other people here.
Martin's voice (*off; loud*) Joshua!
Joshua Who needs people? Dinosaurs are much better.
Martin's voice (*off; louder*) Joshua!
Joshua Did you hear someone calling?
Ronnie Don't you want to see the new baby?
Martin's voice (*off; still louder*) Joshua, Joshua!
Joshua Do you think they'd miss me?
Lucy I wish I had a mum and dad like yours.

Joshua You know what I said about your parents going to Australia? I'm really sorry. I bet they wanted to take you with them.

Lucy No, they didn't. But it's nice of you to say they did. I shouldn't have said that about your mum not loving you any more. That really isn't true. I wish my mum was having a baby.

Joshua You can share mine if you like. Mum won't mind.

Lucy Thanks.

Joshua Uncle Ronnie. Would you mind driving us home? Just to be on the safe side.

Ronnie I'll have a go.

Joshua and Lucy lean into Ronnie and close their eyes

Ronnie Er — let me see now ...

Joshua Think of your imagination as the engine ...

Ronnie Er — right — yes. Well, we — er — we need to go forward, forward to the — er — twentieth century. What have we got? We've got — er — cars, microwave ovens, the international stock exchange ——

Nothing is happening. Uncle Ronnie looks around desperately for inspiration

Joshua People who love us ...

The sound of the time machine begins

Uncle Ronnie Yes, I see — I've got it now. Uncles, aunties, uncles, mums and dads, friends ... Er — hot buttered toast, hugs and kisses, lots of hugs and kisses, lots and lots and lots of hugs and kisses ...

Uncle Ronnie, Joshua and Lucy hurtle forward through time and come to rest in Joshua's bedroom

Auntie Peggy appears. She's been waiting for them

Martín *(off)* Joshua!
Peggy Well, Ronald?

Ronnie hugs Peggy. She is flabbergasted

Ronnie Everything went according to plan. The little sweetheart is safely back with his mummy.

Peggy And the children?

Ronnie hugs the children

Ronnie The children? They're brilliant.
Martin (*off*) Joshua!
Joshua Up here, Dad!
Lucy Wow. I have to go and write a song about that.
Ronnie And I've got a lot of hugging to do.

Ronnie exits

Peggy (*hurrying after Ronnie*) Ronnie, are you all right …? Ronnie, wait for
me!
Lucy Josh? Are you OK?
Joshua You know that song you're going to write? Can I hear it when you've
finished it?
Lucy Sure. Hey. It was a frabjous adventure, wasn't it?
Joshua Yes. Frabjous.
Lucy I'll go back to Auntie Sandra's. There might be a letter from my
mum …

Lucy exits. Martin comes in

Martin Hey, Joshua. I've been looking everywhere for you .

Joshua swings round and hugs his Dad

Joshua Dad! It's great to be back!
Martin I've got some very exciting news.

Martin takes Joshua to Helen's room in the hospital

Helen enters, now dressed in day clothes

Helen and Joshua meet and hug each other

Helen Oh, I've missed you so much!
Joshua I've missed you too, Mum.
Helen I'm coming home now. I'm all packed.
Joshua Right now? This minute?
Helen Right now.
Joshua Great. Let's go then.

Joshua starts to leave. There is the noise of a baby crying. Joshua stops

   Hey Mum. You forgot the baby.
Helen So I did.
Joshua (*gesturing to the Moses basket*) Is it in there?
Martin It's a "she", Josh.
Joshua Is "she" in there?
Helen Yes.
Joshua Can I have a look?
Helen Of course you can.

Martin gives Joshua the baby to hold

Joshua Wow! She's a bit squashed up.
Martin That's what you looked like when you were born.
Joshua She's got such tiny little fingers. She's holding my hand. She's
   holding my hand! Hey Mum, I think she knows who I am.
Helen I think she does.
Martin Shall we go home?
Helen Yes, let's. And Joshua, you and I have to finish our game. You know,
   the one where the oviraptor steals the egg from the mother maiasaura …
Joshua Actually Mum, if you don't mind, I'm a bit tired of dinosaurs. Can
   we play something else?

Lucy, Ronnie and Peggy all come to admire the new baby

*From out of nowhere, they hear the call of the baby dinosaur and the mother's
answering cry*

THE END

FURNITURE AND PROPERTY LIST

On stage: Large beanbag
Model dinosaurs
Box. In it: hoop, skateboard, bendy pipe, toy spade

Off stage: Small electric piano (**Lucy**)
Mobile phone (**Lucy**)
Hot water bottle (**Lucy**)
Pile of neatly-folded washing (**Ronnie**)
Bunch of flowers (**Martin**)
Sheet (**Helen**)
Melted Jaffa cake (**Lucy**)

After **Lucy**'s exit p. 6

Set: "Snow" with egg buried under it. *In egg*: baby dinosaur puppet

After **Lucy**'s exit p. 11

Set: Pile of clothes

Martin takes **Joshua** to **Helen**'s room in the hospital p. 28

Set: "Baby" in Moses basket or car seat

LIGHTING PLOT

Practical fittings required: nil
Various simple settings on an open stage

NB: In the original production of *Joshua's Egg* there were no lighting changes; listed below are cues suggested directly by the text. Individual directors may wish to make more or less use of lighting as circumstances allow

To open: General interior lighting

Cue 1	**Helen** and **Martin** stomp around after **Joshua**	(Page 2)
	Dim lights to night-time setting	

Cue 2	**Joshua** goes back to sleep	(Page 3)
	Brighten lights to morning setting	

Cue 3	**Joshua** devours the maiasaura	(Page 5)
	Lights change to denote time passing	

Cue 4	**Joshua** goes out into the garden	(Page 6)
	Cross-fade to exterior lighting	

Cue 5	**Joshua** runs to the market	(Page 7)
	Cross-fade to another exterior setting	

Cue 6	**Auntie Peggy** exits	(Page 8)
	Dim lights to night-time setting	

Cue 7	**Joshua** goes inside the house; day comes	(Page 11)
	Brighten lights to day-time setting; interior	

Cue 8	**Ronnie** puts **Joshua** to bed	(Page 12)
	Dim lights to night-time setting	

Cue 9	**Maiasaura** exits	(Page 13)
	Brighten lights to morning setting	

Cue 10   **Martin** and **Joshua** get into the lift   (Page 13)
                Cross-fade lights to hospital setting

Cue 11   **Joshua** goes back to his bedroom   (Page 16)
                *Cross-fade lights to **Joshua**'s bedroom setting*

Cue 12   **Peggy**: "Don't stop imagining now!"   (Page 25)
                Time machine lighting

Cue 13   The time machine arrives in prehistory   (Page 25)
                Prehistory lighting

Cue 14   **Uncle Ronnie**: " ... lots of hugs and kisses ..."   (Page 27)
                Time machine lighting

Cue 15   Time machine comes to rest in **Joshua**'s bedroom   (Page 27)
                *Revert to **Joshua**'s bedroom setting*

Cue 16   **Martin** takes **Joshua** to **Helen**'s hospital room   (Page 28)
                Cross-fade lights to hospital setting

EFFECTS PLOT

Cue 1   **Joshua**: "You've broken a promise."   (Page 2)
Car hooter

Cue 2   **Helen**: " ... after the baby's born."   (Page 3)
Hooter

Cue 3   **Uncle Ronnie**: " ... I know exactly what ——"   (Page 11)
Mobile phone rings

Cue 4   **Uncle Ronnie** heads for the door   (Page 22)
Mobile phone rings

Cue 5   **Ronnie**: "Won't!"   (Page 22)
Animal call, loud, distinct, unfamiliar

Cue 6   **Joshua**: "I don't know."   (Page 22)
Animal call as before

Cue 7   **Auntie Peggy** arrives   (Page 22)
Animal call as before

Cue 8   **Ronnie**: " ... if I was poor?"   (Page 24)
Animal call as before

Cue 9   **Joshua**: "Ouch!"   (Page 24)
Animal call as before

Cue 10   **Ronnie, Joshua** and **Lucy** climb out of the   (Page 25)
       time machine
Animal call as before

Cue 11   **Peggy**: "Don't stop imagining now!"   (Page 25)
Whoosh

Cue 12   Time machine arrives in prehistory   (Page 25)
Cut whoosh; bring in strange sounds

Cue 13	**Lucy** and **Joshua** see the tyrannosaurus *Telephone rings ear-splittingly*	(Page 26)
Cue 14	**Joshua**: "People who love us." *Time machine sounds*	(Page 27)
Cue 15	Time machine comes to rest *Cut time machine sounds*	(Page 27)
Cue 16	**Joshua** starts to leave *Baby cries*	(Page 29)
Cue 17	Everyone admires the baby *Call of baby dinosaur;* **Maiasaura**'s *answering cry*	(Page 29)

I Don't Need A Friend

Joshua's Egg

Lyrics: Jacqui Shapiro
Music: Andrew Dodge

♩ = 112

Lucy:

1. I'll
2. I'll
3. I'll

Am   D⁷   F   Fm   C/G   E⁷/G♯

mf   (sim.)

sing you a song of my mo - ther   And the mil - lions of let - ters she sends.
sing you a song of my fa - ther   Of the ma - gi - cal hours- we spend
sing you a song a - bout Lu - cy   A girl who knows how to pre - tend

Am   D⁷   F   Fm⁶

(sim.)

She writes to me twice   Ev - 'ry day which is nice.   In
Sing - ing songs, play - ing games   Think - ing up sil - ly names,   Eat- ing
And I'm miss - ing my mum   And the post does - n't come;   When it

C   E⁷/B   Am   D⁷

all of the world I'm her spe - cia - lest girl. So I....
hot but - tered toast, 'Cos he loves me the most. So I....
does it's not there, No, the let - ter's not there. But I....
Fmaj7 Fm6 C/G E7/B Am C/G
f
cer - tain - ly don't need, I..... def - 'nite - ly don't need,
F C/E F C/E G7/D C
I cer - tain - ly don't... don't need a friend.
F C/E F9/D Fm6 C
mp
Am D7 F Fm6 C/G E7/G♯
mf
(sim.)
Repeat & fade

Adventures With Lucy

Joshua's Egg

Lyrics: Jacqui Shapiro
Music: Andrew Dodge

1. I'm on-ly five and a quar-ter, My name is Lu - - cy Snow.
2. Bat- man he's - got Ro- bin, Or he wouldn't be brave - - and bold.

You think I'm just - - a ba - by, But you should know all the
E - - ven - Super- girl gets ner - vous With- out a friend - ly -

things I know.. ..ow   You can own a skate-board or
hand to ho - old.   cer-tain to get lone-ly or

C   F/C   B♭/C   C   F/C B♭/C C   Dm

a - ny   toy   you   like,   But ad - ven - tures aren't for own - ing like your
frigh - tened   in the   end,   But if   you   share   your ad - ven - ture   I

C   G

Le - go   set or   three   speed   bike.
promise I'll be your   best - est   friend.   You've

B♭m   C   A⁷

got to take some- bo - dy with you; Now who could that some- bo - dy be?

Dm

f

Ad - ven - tures are bet - ter with Lu - cy. You've

F

1.

2.

met her: She's me! me!

Gm⁷ A⁷ Dm Dm

Time Machine

Joshua's Egg

Lyrics: Jacqui Shapiro
Music: Andrew Dodge

been on a bus, flied on a plane, Been sick on a boat, thrown up on a plane -- I've

e- ven ri- ded my bike in the rain, But there's some- thing e- ven bet- ter let me ex - plain — You

won't be lieve — The sights you'll see — In a
How far you flew —

time ma-chine — time ma-chine — time, time, time ma-chine — You

won't be lieve the sights you'll see in a time ma-chine that goes: Whoosh, wham,
how far you flew Bim. bam.

Last Time.

whoosh, wham, wheeeeee!
bim, bam, whoooo!
2. If you

VERSE 2

want to see a real live di-no-saur, Use a time ma-chine 'cos that's what it's for —

Press those but-tons it'-ll go with a roar, Take you on a pre-his-to-ric tour — You

BACK TO 𝄋

VERSE 3

Some-times I think sort of slow, 'Cos I'm on-ly five, but still I know — Some

things you learn you've got to let go, Take the egg to the Ma-ma, let the ba-by grow — You

BACK TO 𝄋

Think Back

Joshua's Egg

Lyrics: Jacqui Shapiro
Music: Andrew Dodge

1. Think back to the time When they sent you a - way, When —
2. Think back to the crying, The time of sting - ing tears, And the
3. Think back to the boy And the man — — he be - came Who —

you lay all a - lone In a world — — cold and grey.
child — — in the night who — no — — bo - dy hears.
knows — — how to hear A — child — — who's in pain.

The pain in your heart was as big as the sky — — You —
Re- mem - ber the wan - ting The sobs and the sighs — — The —
The ba - by is cal - l-ng And here is the man — — Who —

G   D/F#   F#7   Bm7

mf

tried to be tough, But you wan - ted to cry.
e - cho - ing silence That — — gree - ted his cries.
lis - tens and waits, With its life in his hands.

E7   G7   D/F#

mp

Think back to the time

Em7   D/F#   G9   D/F#

p

Think back to the time

REPEAT & FADE

Em7   D/F#   G9   G9/A   A